# GROWING UP
## *with Jesus*

**THE MUFFIN FAMILY**

**GROWING UP WITH GOD SERIES** ®

# V. GILBERT BEERS
*Illustrated by* HELEN ENDRES

**HARVEST HOUSE PUBLISHERS**
Eugene, Oregon 97402

**GROWING UP WITH JESUS**

Copyright © 1987 by V. Gilbert Beers
Published by Harvest House Publishers
Eugene, Oregon 97402

Library of Congress Catalog Card
   Number 87-081043
ISBN 0-89081-525-9

**Printed in the United States of America.**

# BEFORE YOU READ

GROWING UP WITH JESUS will help your child grow up and grow strong with Jesus. Jesus is the Savior, the only one who can show your child the way to God. But He is also a loving Friend who walks beside your child each day. Growing up with Jesus is the only right way to grow up!

This book is part of the Muffin Family series, GROWING UP WITH GOD. Each story is really two stories—a Bible story, with a Bible truth about the way Jesus walked and talked on earth and how He touched lives, and a Muffin Family story which shows how Jesus walks with an ordinary family today.

The Muffin Family is a family much like you want your family to be. Like the rest of us, they are not perfect, but they solve their problems the way Jesus' friends should.

Each Bible story/Muffin story couplet works together as a team. The truth seen in the Bible story is lived out in the daily lives of the Muffin Family. It is a truth about moral and spiritual values—*forgiveness, kindness, love, thankfulness,* and others.

At the end of each Bible story/Muffin story couplet you will find two pages of Muffin application, to help you and your child apply the Bible teaching and moral/spiritual value to YOUR child's life.

A color-coding system helps you find your way through this book. The book has four sections, "Growing up to Love Jesus," "Growing up to Follow Jesus," "Growing up to Please Jesus," and "Growing up to Praise Jesus." Each of these sections has a different identifying color that begins on the contents pages and continues throughout that section.

Bible stories have a color-coded line around the margin. Muffin Family stories have a color-coded bar at the bottom. Muffin application pages have a color-coded line around the pages. Labels at the bottom of the pages identify Bible story, Muffin Family story, and Muffin application pages.

---

The Muffin Family Growing Up With God series consists of:

> **Growing Up With Jesus**
> **Growing Up With My Family**
> **Growing Up to Praise God**
> **Growing Up With God's Friends**

# TO PARENTS AND TEACHERS

More than anything else, you want your child to come to know Jesus personally. In a world that sends confusing signals to our children about the way to live, we need to help them know God's Word and what He says about Jesus.

This is a book about people who walked with Jesus and came to know Him. Some lived in Bible times. The Muffin Family and their friends are people much like us.

Bible stories are retold in the language and thought of today. Bible people come alive so that your child feels at home with them. Bible truth also comes alive. What Maxi Muffin learns is not much different from what Peter learned.

Sometimes you will see a make-believe story, a touch of fantasy. We clearly mark these stories so that your child will not confuse real life and fantasy. But fantasy is important in growing up.

So come with The Muffin Family into exciting adventures that will change your child's life. You'll be glad you did.

# What You
# Will Find
# in This Book

## GROWING UP
## TO PLEASE JESUS

## GROWING UP
## TO PRAISE JESUS

# GROWING UP
## TO LOVE JESUS

# It's Easy to Love Jesus

**Mark 5:21-34**

"Help me!"

"Teach me!"

"Heal me!"

Everywhere Jesus went, people crowded around Him. They begged Him to help.

One day Jesus and His friends were sailing home to Capernaum. Crowds came to meet Him.

"Help me!" someone said.

"Teach me!" said another.

"Heal me!" someone else said.

The people crowded around Jesus' boat as He got out. They squeezed closer to get to Him when He stepped on shore.

Jesus looked around. There were so many who needed help. So many needed healing. And He needed to tell everyone about God and His home.

Who should be first?

Suddenly Jesus stopped. He looked from person to person.

"Who touched My clothes?" He asked.

Jesus' friends were surprised. "Everyone is squeezing close to You," they said, "Why are You asking who touched Your clothes?"

But Jesus still looked at the people around Him. He knew someone had touched His clothes to be healed.

The crowd became quiet as a woman came toward Jesus. She fell on her knees, bowing before Him. Trembling and afraid, she told Jesus her story.

For twelve years she had suffered with a sore that would not stop bleeding. She had spent all her money, going from doctor to doctor. But no one could help her. Instead, she got worse.

Then the woman had heard that Jesus was coming. "If only I can touch the fringe at the bottom of His cloak, I will be healed," she had said.

The woman believed that so much that she moved through the crowd to get to Jesus. In a moment of faith, she reached out and touched the fringe of His cloak. At that moment she was healed.

Jesus smiled at the woman with so much faith. "Your faith has healed you," Jesus told her. "Your sickness is gone. You are well."

The woman was too happy to speak. But as Jesus turned to go, her heart sang with joy. She had a new life, and she loved Jesus for giving it to her.

# It's Hard to Love a Greedy King

"Why such a cheerful face, Maxi?"

"Don't be cute, Mini. I'm so broke I can't even buy a chocolate sundae."

Maxi looked like Mr. Gloom as he sat on the old stump, with his chin in his hands.

"I wish I could be King Midas," said Maxi. "You remember, he was the king that turned everything he touched to gold. Wow! Wouldn't that be fun for one day. I could get rich."

"Your family and friends would certainly stay away from you," said Mini.

Maxi was still thinking about King Midas when he went to bed that night. Maxi set his alarm for the next morning.

"KA-ZOOM!" Maxi said as he touched the clock. "If I had the golden touch I would have a golden clock! That would buy a thousand chocolate sundaes."

Maxi reached up to turn off his lamp. "KA-ZAM!" he said. "A golden lamp would buy two thousand chocolate sundaes."

Before long, Maxi had drifted off to sleep. He dreamed that he was King Maxi Midas and that he really did have the golden touch.

"KA-ZOOM!" Some flowers turned to gold. "KA-ZAM!" A tree and bush became pure gold.

Maxi was so busy KA-ZAM-ing and KA-ZOOM-ing that he didn't hear Mini ride up on her horse.

"What's going on?" Mini asked.

"We're rich!" said King Maxi Midas. "Let's go down to Pop's Sweet Shop and I'll buy

you a chocolate sundae as big as a house."

"That sounds wonderful," said Mini. "Jump on my horse with me and we'll go now."

But as soon as King Maxi Midas jumped on the horse with Mini—KA-ZAM!—both Mini and her horse turned into a golden statue.

"OH, NO!" shouted Maxi. "Mini has turned to gold. What will I do?"

Maxi forgot about turning things to gold and ran to the palace as fast as he could go, leaving behind a trail of golden statues of bowing guards.

"Mommi! Poppi! Something terrible has happened to Mini," King Maxi Midas shouted. Then without thinking he threw his arms around them. KA-ZOOM! KA-ZAM! There were golden statues of Mommi and Poppi.

Before Maxi could say a word, he felt the royal dog and cat rub against him. Suddenly Ruff and Tuff were golden statues.

"MOMMI! POPPI! MINI! RUFF! TUFF!" King Maxi Midas kept shouting again and again.

Maxi felt a warm hand on him. "Don't touch me!" he shouted. "You'll turn to gold."

"I hope not," Mommi whispered softly. "Then who would wake you when you have bad dreams?"

Maxi's eyes fluttered. Mommi, Poppi, Mini, Ruff, and Tuff were all there. "Oh, my wonderful family," he said. "You're worth more to me than all the gold in the world."

"That's a lot of chocolate sundaes," said Poppi. "Are you sure we're worth that much?"

"MUCH more!" said Maxi. "MUCH, MUCH more."

# Growing Is . . .
# Loving Jesus

### What the Bible Story Teaches
We should love Jesus because of who He is and what He does for us.

### Thinking about the Bible Story
1. What trouble did the sick woman have?
2. How did Jesus help her?
3. Why do you think she loved Jesus? Would you love Jesus if you were this woman? Why?

### What the Muffin Story Teaches
We should love our family more than money. And we should love Jesus more than money.

### Thinking about the Muffin Story
1. Why did Maxi want to be King Midas? What did he want to do with "the golden touch"?
2. In his dream, how did Maxi and his family get hurt by his golden touch?
3. How did Maxi come to love his family very much? Do you love your family more than money? Do you love Jesus more than money? Why?

# How Do You Show Jesus That You Love Him?

Which would show Jesus that you love Him?

1. Going to church
2. Reading your Bible
3. Arguing with your family
4. Loving your family
5. Talking with Jesus
6. Obeying what Jesus says

## The Bible Says

*Jesus said, "If you love Me you will obey Me"* (from John 14:15).

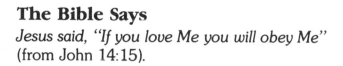

## Prayer

Dear Jesus, I love You. Teach me to show my love by doing what You want. Amen.

# Do You Love Me Enough to Care?

**Mark 10:13-16**

"You can't bring those children here!" the disciples told some mothers and fathers. "Don't you see how busy Jesus is?"

The mothers and fathers certainly did see how busy Jesus was. People were crowding around Him on every side. The blind wanted to see. The crippled wanted to walk. The sick were begging Jesus to heal them.

"Go away," the disciples said. "Jesus is busy."

"But we want to see Jesus," the children said.

Before long everyone was talking loud to each other. Then Jesus came to see what was going on. "What is the matter?" He asked.

"These people have brought their children to see You," said the disciples. "We told them to go away. You are too busy."

Jesus smiled at the children. He knew how much they wanted to see Him.

"Let the children come to Me," said Jesus. "You must not send them away. Anyone who wants to go to heaven must first become like one of them."

The disciples were surprised. Then they remembered that these children believed in Jesus with all their hearts. Many of the people in the crowd did not believe in Jesus like these children did. Their hearts were still hard and cold. No wonder Jesus said that they must become like little children.

So the crowd of older people waited while Jesus talked with the children. For a while, the sick would wait to be healed. The crippled would wait to walk. The blind would wait to see.

Jesus wanted to spend time now with His special friends, the children. Everything else would wait.

Jesus will listen to you at any time. Why not talk to Him right now?

# Do You Love Me Enough to Listen?

"Poppi. Do you love me?"

"Uh huh."

"Will you do something special for me?"

"Uh huh."

Poppi was reading his newspaper. And when Poppi was doing that, he really wasn't listening. He loved Mini Muffin. But he just wasn't listening.

"Poppi. Would you still love me if I brought a friend home?"

"Uh huh."

"But he's a big friend with a lot of hair. Is that OK?"

"Uh huh."

"And he barks and has to be fed. You'll help me feed him, won't you?"

"Uh huh."

"Oh, Poppi, that's wonderful. He's so lonely. Someone has dumped him out and he has no place to go. May I keep him forever?"

"Uh huh."

"Thank you, Poppi. Thank you. I'll go get him right now. Is it OK to bring him here in the living room?"

"Uh huh."

"OK, Poppi. You wait right here and I'll be back soon. You'll stay here until we get back won't you?"

"Uh huh."

Mini Muffin ran from the house as fast as she could go. She ran down the street to find her big hairy friend that barked and had to be fed.

"There you are, Buster," Mini said at last. "You're coming home with me. You can be Ruff's big brother."

Buster tagged along behind Mini. He followed her into the house and through the living room to Poppi. Poppi was still reading his newspaper.

"Poppi, my friend Buster is here. You said he could stay with us, didn't you?"

"Uh huh."

"Buster, give Poppi a big love."

Buster poked his head up under Poppi's newspaper and slurped Poppi's nose with his big tongue.

"YEOOOWWWW!" Poppi shouted,

jumping from his chair. "Get that monster out of here! He's attacking me." Buster just stood there, wagging his tail.

"But Poppi, you told me I could bring him here and keep him forever," said Mini. "You said you would help me feed him." Mini told Poppi all the other "Uh huhs" he had said.

Poppi hung his head. "I'm sorry, Mini. I was too busy with my newspaper. I didn't hear a word you said."

Mini thought for a minute. "You do love me, don't you Poppi? You do love me more than your newspaper," she asked.

"Yes, I really do," said Poppi. "And I love you enough to listen more carefully next time. But now I will help you find Buster the right home."

From that time on, Poppi listened carefully to Mini. After all, what might she bring next?

# owing Is . . .
## istening

### What the Bible Story Teaches

When you care about someone you will take time to listen to that person. Jesus did!

### Thinking about the Bible Story

1. Who wanted to talk with Jesus? Why?
2. Why did Jesus' friends think He would not have time for the children?
3. How did Jesus show that He wanted to talk with the children and listen to them?

### What the Muffin Story Teaches

Loving is listening. When you love someone, you will listen to that person.

### Thinking about the Muffin Story

1. Was Poppi really listening to Mini? How do you know?
2. How would the story have been different if he really had listened?
3. Why should we listen to those we love?

# Will You Listen More Carefully Now?

Which of these people is listening?

1. Mini is telling Mommi what happened at school today. Mommi asks Mini to tell her more.
2. Poppi is telling Mommi what happened at work today. Mommi keeps on reading her book.
3. Maxi tells Poppi about a bully down the street. Poppi doesn't say anything.
4. Mommi says her back is hurting. Maxi says "I'm sorry."

## The Bible Says

*Jesus said, "My people listen to Me!"* (from John 10:27).

## Prayer

Dear Jesus, You always listen to me. Teach me to listen to You and my family. Amen.

# GROWING UP
# TO FOLLOW JESUS

# Following Jesus

**John 1:35-51**

"Look, there is God's Son," John the Baptist said to two of his friends. John pointed to Jesus.

Jesus was God's Son. He was no ordinary man. Only God's Son could die for our sins. Only God's Son could show us the way to God.

"Let's go," said one of the friends. So the two of them hurried after Jesus. They wanted to follow Him and learn what He would say.

"What do you want?" Jesus asked when He saw them coming.

"We want to go home with You so You can teach us," they said.

"Come with Me," said Jesus. They went with Jesus to the place where He was staying. They stayed with Him all afternoon, listening to Him tell about His real home in heaven. Most important they listened to Jesus tell how they could go to live there if they would follow Him.

Andrew, one of these two men, went to find his brother Simon. He was excited. He was sure now that Jesus was God's Son. He wanted Simon to meet Jesus and hear Him too.

"We have found Him!" Andrew shouted when he found Simon.

"Found who?" asked Simon.

"God's Son!" said Andrew. "Come with me and meet Him. I know you will want to follow Him."

Simon went with Andrew to meet Jesus. "You will follow Me," Jesus told Simon when He looked into his face. "From now on you will be called Peter." This new name meant "a rock."

The next day Jesus met a man named Philip. "Come and be My follower," Jesus told him.

Philip was so excited to become Jesus' follower that he ran to find his friend Nathanael. "We have found God's Son!" he shouted. "His name is Jesus. He is from Nazareth."

"That town?" Nathanael asked. "How can God's Son come from there?" Nazareth wasn't an exciting town as you can see.

"Come and meet Him," said Philip. "See for yourself."

Nathanael went with Philip. He must have grumbled a little as he went.

"Here comes a good man," Jesus said when He met Nathanael.

"How do you know?" Nathanael asked.

"I know all about you," said Jesus. "I saw you sitting under that fig tree before Philip found you." Nathanael stared at Jesus. How could He know that? Jesus really must be God's Son.

Jesus had four followers now—Peter, Andrew, Philip and Nathanael. With His four followers He went toward Galilee.

Later eight more men would follow Jesus. These twelve would become known as the Twelve Disciples. Sometimes they are called The Apostles. These men went everywhere Jesus went. Someday they would teach many others to follow Jesus.

# Follow the King's Son

A Make-believe Story Poppi Told Maxi and Mini about the Muffkins who Live in Muffkinland

"Where are you going?" asked the Muffkin with the little tin horn.

"To see the king!" said the Muffkin with the booming drum. "Come on! We'll have a parade."

"Where are you going?" asked the Muffkin with the cymbals.

"To see the king!" said the Muffkins with the booming drum and the little tin horn. "Come on! We'll have a parade."

"Where are you going?" asked the Muff-kin with the cymbals.

"To see the king!" said the Muffkins with the booming drum and the little tin horn. "Come on! We'll have a parade."

"Where are you going?" asked the Muff-kin with the wooden baton.

"To see the king!" said the Muffkins with the booming drum, the little tin horn, and the cymbals. "Come on! We'll have a parade."

"Where are you going?" asked the Muff-kin with the bright little flag.

"To see the king!" said the Muffkins with the booming drum, the little tin horn, the cymbals, and the wooden baton. "Come on! We'll have a parade."

"Where are you going?" asked the little Ruffkin dog and the little Tuffkin cat.

"To see the king!" said the Muffkins with

the booming drum, the little tin horn, the cymbals, the wooden baton, and the bright little flag. "Come on! We'll have a parade."

"Where are you going?" asked the king's son, who sat by the side of the road.

"To see the king!" said the Muffkins. By this time they had a parade with the drum booming, the horn tooting, the cymbals clanging, the wooden baton twirling, and the bright little flag waving.

"Why don't you follow me?" said the king's son. "I'm going home soon. If you follow me you will see the king."

"Oh, no," said the Muffkins on parade.

"You should follow us instead. You don't have drums booming, horns tooting, cymbals clanging, batons twirling or flags waving. How can you find your way to the king without these things?"

The Muffkins on parade boomed and tooted. They clanged and twirled. And they waved the bright little flag. But all they did was march around and around a big tree. The little Ruffkin dog and little Tuffkin cat marched around and around with them.

The king's son watched by the side of the road. He watched the parade go around and around. But he saw that it was not going to the king.

At last the king's son sadly left and went home. There the king was waiting to have dinner with him.

# Growing Is . . . Following Jesus

### What the Bible Story Teaches

We should follow Jesus because He is the only one who knows the way to God.

### Thinking about the Bible Story

1. Who were the four men who followed Jesus?
2. Why do you think they followed Him?
3. How did they help others learn to follow Him?

### What the Muffin Story Teaches

If you want to see the king you should follow the king's son home. If you want to go to God's home some day you should follow His Son.

### Thinking about the Muffin Story

1. Where did the Muffkins want to go?
2. Why didn't they get to see the king?
3. How could they have gone to see him?
4. Why should you follow Jesus?

# Which of These Friends Follow Jesus?

Maxi's and Mini's friends are following Jesus when:

1. Pookie says, "I don't want to read the Bible."
2. BoBo says, "I'll be glad to go to Sunday school today."
3. Maria says, "I want to do what I want."
4. Charlie says, "Let me tell you about Jesus."
5. Tony says, "Why talk to Jesus when you can't see Him?"

## The Bible Says

*Jesus said, "Follow Me"* (from Mark 1:17).

## Prayer

Dear Jesus, You know the way to Your home in heaven. Thanks for letting me follow You. Amen.

# Listen to Jesus!

**Luke 10:38-42**

"Martha! Martha! Look who is coming!" Mary called.

Martha was excited to see Jesus coming toward their house. She and Mary were always excited when He came to Bethany.

But before Jesus reached their door, Martha began to worry about lunch. "What will I feed Him?" she wondered. "And look at the house. I must clean up before He gets here."

Martha was so busy cleaning and fixing and fussing that she hardly had time to say hello. Then as soon as she did, she ran to the kitchen.

Mary didn't care much about lunch. She didn't even care if she ate lunch. She would rather talk with Jesus. She had so many questions to ask.

Martha rushed around the kitchen, filling pots with water and stirring kettles of food. She clattered and banged things around without hearing a word Jesus said.

Suddenly Martha realized she was doing all the work while Mary was doing nothing. At last she came into the room where Mary sat by Jesus' feet, listening carefully.

"Lord, doesn't it bother You that my sister lets me do all the work?" she asked. It was a bit rude to ask an important guest such a question, but she did it anyway.

You might think that Jesus would ask Mary to help Martha. But He really did not care if He ate lunch either.

"Martha, don't you see that Mary wants to listen to Me, and that is better than eating," Jesus answered.

Did Mary help Martha? We don't know. But we do know that Mary learned to follow Jesus by listening to Him. That's good for us to learn too isn't it?

# Better than Pirate Treasure

"Grandmommi! What an exciting attic you have!" Mini almost shouted.

"Yeah, it's full of old things," Maxi added. "Where did you get all these things?"

Grandmommi laughed. "When you live in one house all these years, a lot of things find their way to the attic."

Maxi and Mini looked at an old butter churn. They saw old lamps and chairs and a bird cage.

"What's in that old chest?" Maxi asked.

"That's our treasure chest," Grandmommi said with a twinkle in her eye.

"TREASURE CHEST?" Maxi asked, his mouth falling open. "Is it full of old gold coins and stuff from a pirate ship?"

"Not quite," said Grandmommi. "Who wants stuffy old coins and pirate treasure?"

"I do," said Maxi.

"The treasure in that chest is worth more than pirate treasure," said Grandmommi.

Maxi's eyes grew big like saucers.

"It must be worth a fortune," he whispered to Mini. "Maybe it's diamonds and rubies."

"What IS it, Grandmommi?" Mini asked.

Grandmommi laughed. "Treasure isn't always money," she said softly. "Some of our richest treasures can't be spent at the store."

"May we see your treasure, Grandmommi?" Maxi asked.

"Yes, open the lid," she said.

Mini and Maxi opened the lid slowly. "There's nothing but old books and clothes," said Maxi. "I don't see any treasure."

"Let's look closer," said Grandmommi.

"This is my wedding dress. I wore it when Grandpoppi and I were married."

"May I put it on?" Mini asked.

"Of course," said Grandmommi.

Mini wiggled into the old dress and looked at herself in a big mirror leaning against an old dresser. She giggled as she saw herself in the old-fashioned wedding dress.

"Lovely bride!" said Grandmommi.

"Yuk," said Maxi.

Grandmommi took an old photo album from the chest. "Family treasures," she said softly. "Pictures of my grandmother and grandfather and their families."

More family treasures came from the chest. There was a gold watch Grandpoppi's father got as a Christmas gift many years before. And a beautiful quilt Grandmommi's mother had made.

"Here is one of my greatest treasures of all," said Grandmommi as she took out a small white Bible. When I was a little girl, I read from this Bible every day. I memorized verses from this. And with this Bible my poppi helped me accept Jesus as my Savior. He helped me know that Jesus is the best treasure of all."

Maxi and Mini were quiet for a while as they looked through the Bible. They smiled as they saw a picture of Grandmommi when she was a little girl, holding the Bible.

"You're right, Grandmommi," Maxi said with a smile.

"About what?" asked Grandmommi.

"These treasures really are worth much more than a chest full of pirate gold," said Maxi.

"I think so too," said Mini. "And I'm going to save the Bible I'm reading to show my grandchildren. I want them to know that Jesus is more important than all the pirate treasure in the world."

Maxi and Grandmommi smiled as they thought of Mini's grandchildren. Wouldn't you?

But everyone was glad that they could follow Jesus. Wouldn't you rather follow Jesus than have all the pirate treasure in the world?

# Growing Is . . .
# Being Glad for Jesus

## What the Bible Story Teaches

Sometimes we should sit and talk with Jesus instead of rushing around trying to do something for Him.

## Thinking about the Bible Story

1. What did Martha want to do for Jesus?
2. What did Mary want to do with Jesus?
3. Why did Jesus want Mary to keep on talking and listening?

## What the Muffin Story Teaches

We should be more thankful for our family than a chest full of gold. That's why it's more important to spend time with our family than to try to get a lot of money.

## Thinking about the Muffin Story

1. What kind of treasure did Grandmommi have in the big chest?
2. Why did Maxi say these were treasures worth more than gold?
3. Would you trade your family for a chest full of gold? Why not?

# What Do You Like to Do with Your Family?

When your family does things together, which do you like to do?

1. Play games.
2. Go on picnics.
3. Argue and fight.
4. Eat meals together.
5. Talk about Jesus.
6. Talk about fun things.

## The Bible Says

*It is good and it is fun to live together and do special things together* (from Psalm 133:1)

## Prayer

Dear Jesus, thank You for letting me listen to You and talk with You. And thank You for helping us do that as a family. Amen.

# Follow Me!

**Luke 5:1-11**

"Catch some fish, Peter," Jesus said.

"We've tried all night," Peter answered. "But we didn't catch one fish."

"Throw your nets over there," Jesus said.

Peter and his fishermen friends had thrown their nets from this fishing boat all night. Why do it again? But if Jesus said to do it, he would do it.

Once more Peter and his friends threw out their nets. The water bubbled and splashed. Their nets were full of fish.

"Follow me," Jesus said when Peter and his brother Andrew reached shore.

"I have been following You," Peter must have said. Peter and Andrew often went with Jesus to listen to Him teach. They often watched Him heal.

But this time Jesus was asking these two fishermen to leave their fishing boats. He was asking them to leave their nets. He was asking them to leave the fish.

"Come with Me, and I will teach you how to fish for people," Jesus said.

From now on, Peter and Andrew would not throw their fishing nets from boats. From now on they would not catch fish and sell them to make a living. From now on they would help other people love Jesus and follow Him. That's what Jesus meant when He said they would fish for people.

Do you ever fish for people? You do whenever you help a friend love Jesus and follow Him.

# Which Way?

A Make-believe Story that Mommi Told Mini and Maxi about Mini's Stuffed Animals on Thimblelane Trails.

"Which is the right way home?" Maxi wondered.

"It could be this way," said Mini. "Or it could be that way."

Mini and Maxi had been walking along Thimblelane Trails with Buffy Bear. But now it was time to go home.

But which way was the right way? Maxi and Mini and Buffy Bear stood at a place where one road went this way. The other road went that way.

"So which is the right way?" Maxi asked again.

"My way," a voice croaked. There was Todie, sitting beside the left trail.

"If you go left you will be right," said Todie. "But if you go right you will be left in the wrong place."

"Don't listen to him," said Buffy Bear. "The right trail is the right trail."

"Listen! I know these trails like the back of my hand," said Todie. Then he took out a big card and stuck it in his cap.

"GUIDE," Mini read. "Are you a guide, Todie?"

"The very best," said Todie. "Follow me."

"Don't," said Buffy Bear. "He will lead you the wrong way. Follow me."

Maxi and Mini looked confused. They weren't sure which one to follow.

"Do you have a special guide's card?" Todie asked Buffy Bear.

Buffy Bear leaned against a tree to think about that. He knew that Todie had made his own card. But it was a card and he didn't have one. And he was leaning against a tree and Todie wasn't.

"Let's go!" said Todie. He seemed so sure of himself that Maxi and Mini followed.

"Oh, dear," said Buffy Bear. "This is wrong. I know it."

Before long Maxi and Mini knew it was wrong too. Thimblelane Trails stopped. They were at the edge of a pond. Todie kept on going, jumping from one lily pad to another.

"Wait," Mini called to Todie. "I thought you said this was the right way home."

"Home?" said Todie. "Who said anything about home? This is the right way to the pond. Follow me."

But Mini and Maxi and Buffy Bear were already on their way back where the roads crossed. This time they would follow Buffy Bear. This time they would follow the right way home.

# Growing Is . . . Going the Right Way

### What the Bible Story Teaches

Jesus' way is the right way. Sometimes we may have to give up something important to follow Him in His way.

### Thinking about the Bible Story

1. What kind of work did Peter and Andrew do?
2. Why did they leave their fishing business?
3. What would they do for Jesus?

### What the Muffin Story Teaches

Follow the person who knows the right way.

### Thinking about the Muffin Story

1. Why did Maxi and Mini follow Todie?
2. Where did they want to go? Where did he lead them?
3. When you want to know the way to heaven, who should you follow? Do you?

# How Does Jesus Know the Way to Heaven?

## Which of these is true?

1. Jesus lived in heaven before He came to earth.
2. Someone gave Jesus a map to show Him the way.
3. Jesus is God's Son, so He knows God's home.

## The Bible Says

*Jesus said, "I am the way . . . no one can come to God except by following Me"* (from John 14:6).

## Prayer

Dear Jesus, thank You for telling me about Your wonderful home in heaven. Thank You for showing me the way. Amen.

# GROWING UP
## TO PLEASE JESUS

# How to Please Jesus

**Matthew 3:13-17; Mark 1:9-11**

Have you ever heard of John the Baptist? He was a different kind of man. If he went to work with your father, everyone would stare at him.

John lived out in the wilderness. He preached there. He didn't dress up like other people. Instead he wore rough clothes.

John was Jesus' cousin. But John knew that Jesus was more than just a cousin. He knew that Jesus was God's Son.

One day Jesus came out to the wilderness to see John. He watched John baptizing people. These people had asked God to forgive their sins. When they did, John baptized them in the Jordan River.

"Baptize Me, too," Jesus told John.

John did not want to do this. He knew that Jesus had never sinned. So Jesus never had to ask God to forgive Him. Why did He need to be baptized?

"No, You should baptize me instead," John answered. "Why should I baptize You?"

Jesus explained to John that this was part of God's plan for Him. God wanted Jesus to be baptized. We don't know why. But we know that God wanted Him to do it.

And Jesus wanted to do it.

When John saw that this would please Jesus, he baptized Jesus in the Jordan River. It's a good idea to please Jesus, even when we don't know why He wants us to do something.

When Jesus came up out of the water, the Spirit of God came down like a dove. "This is My Son. I love Him. I am pleased with Him," a voice said.

It was God's voice. Wouldn't you like God to say that He loves you and is pleased with you? You can if you will please Jesus.

# The Pleasing Jesus Barometer

"Why did the weatherman on TV say partly cloudy?" Mini's friend Maria asked.

"What should he say?" Maria's poppi asked.

"Partly sunny!" said Maria. "Partly cloudy sounds gloomy. Partly sunny sounds happy."

"Hmmm. We should have you write the weather forecasts," said Maria's poppi.

"Clouds are like frowns and suns are like smiles," said Maria. "When I smile my weather is sunny. When I frown my weather is cloudy."

"Why don't you make a barometer to hang on the wall," said Maria's poppi. "You can use smiling paper suns and frowning clouds."

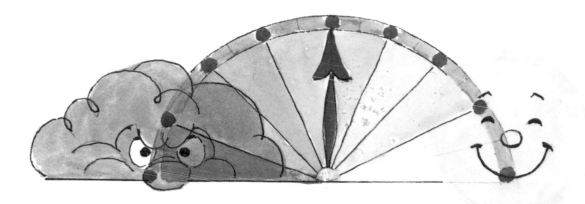

"Oh, Poppi! That's a wonderful idea," said Maria. "I'll make a Pleasing Poppi Barometer. When I please you and help you smile I'll put up a little sun picture on it. When I don't please you and make you sad, I'll put up a little cloud picture."

"How about a Pleasing Jesus Barometer?" said Maria's poppi. "I want you to please me and I would love to have a Pleasing Poppi Barometer. But if you please Jesus, you will also please me."

Maria thought about that for a little while. "When I please Jesus do I always please you?" she asked.

"Yes you do," said Maria's poppi. "All the things that Jesus wants you to do are things that I want you to do."

"Will you help me make my Pleasing Jesus Barometer, Poppi?" Maria asked.

"I think that would please Jesus, don't you?" Maria's poppi said with a laugh.

Do you think it would be fun to make a Pleasing Jesus Barometer? Do you think that would please your mommi and poppi if you pleased Jesus? We do.

# Growing Is . . .
# Pleasing Jesus

### What the Bible Story Teaches
God is pleased with Jesus. Let's live so that God is also pleased with us.

### Thinking about the Bible Story
1. Why did Jesus want John to baptize Him?
2. Who spoke from heaven?
3. What did God say about Jesus?

### What the Muffin Story Teaches
When we please Jesus, that will usually please our parents too.

### Thinking about the Muffin Story
1. What kind of barometer did Maria want to make?
2. What would this barometer show?
3. Would Maria please her poppi if she pleased Jesus first? Why?
4. Would you like to please Jesus? Why?

# Why Do You Want to Please Jesus?

Do you want to please Jesus? Why do you want to do that?

1. Because I will get rich.
2. Because I will be famous.
3. Because my parents will be glad.
4. Because that's what Jesus wants.
5. Because the Bible says I should.

## The Bible Says

*Jesus said, "My friends do what I ask"* (from John 14:15).

## Prayer

Dear Jesus, whenever I please You I feel like putting a little paper sun on my wall. Be with me so that I can put many little paper suns on my wall. Amen.

## Pleasing Jesus by What We Do

**Luke 19:1-10**

Nobody liked Zacchaeus. He was rich. He had a beautiful home. He had lots of money. But he was a tax collector. Nobody liked tax collectors. They made people pay taxes. They also cheated the people and made them pay much more than their taxes.

Zacchaeus got richer while the people he cheated got poorer. Now you know why he had no friends.

One day Zacchaeus heard that Jesus was coming. He had heard many wonderful things about Jesus. Perhaps Jesus would be his friend.

When Zacchaeus saw a big crowd coming down the road he knew that Jesus was in the middle. That's the way it was. People always crowded around Jesus wherever He went.

Zacchaeus ran toward the crowd. But he was a short man. He could not see Jesus.

Then Zacchaeus had an idea. He climbed into a sycamore tree. He sat on a big branch.

When Jesus came under the tree He saw Zacchaeus. "Zacchaeus, come down from there," Jesus said. "I want to stay at your house today."

Zacchaeus was excited and happy. Jesus wanted to be his friend.

But when Jesus came to his house, Zacchaeus began to think about all the bad things he had done. He knew he could not really be Jesus' friend until he stopped doing these bad things.

"I'm going to stop cheating people," Zacchaeus told Jesus. "I will pay the people I have cheated four times as much as I took from them. I also will give half of all I own to poor people."

Jesus was glad to hear that. He knew now that Zacchaeus wanted to follow Him and please Him.

It isn't enough to just say we want to please Jesus, is it? If we really want to please Him, we must DO what pleases Him. That's something you should remember today when you tell Jesus, "I want to please You."

# Pleasing Jesus by What We Don't Do

A Muffin Make-believe Story that Poppi Told to Mini and Maxi about Rainbow Island

Have you ever been to Rainbow Island? It's a wonderful place you can visit with Maxi and Mini. But you do have to pretend that you're there, don't you?

Maxi and Mini love to visit Rainbow Island with its Pippins and Painted Ponies. But they also love to come home. In this story Maxi and Mini are ready to sail home after a wonderful visit. After they said good-bye to the Painted Ponies and the boy who took care of them, Mini and Maxi said good-bye to the Pippins.

"Thank you, thank you for coming to see us," the Peppermint Pippin said to Maxi and Mini.

"We want to give you a special going away gift," said the Gingerbread Pippin.

"Something that you can't get back in your hometown," said the Gumdrop Pippin.

"So close your eyes and when you open them you will see a surprise," said the Lolli-pop Pippin.

Mini and Maxi closed their eyes. When they opened them the Pippins shouted "Surprise! Surprise!"

There were four little treasure chests. In one little chest were the most beautiful peppermint sticks Mini and Maxi had ever seen. In

another were the most wonderful gumdrops they had ever seen. In the third were the best lollipops you can imagine. And in the last was the most charming gingerbread of all.

"Take some from each chest," said the Peppermint Pippin.

Maxi's eyes sparkled. His eyes grew big like saucers.

"Thank you, thank you," said Mini. She took one piece from each chest and put them into a little bag the Pippins gave her.

Maxi took one from each chest too. But his eyes still sparkled and looked big like saucers. So he took another from each chest. Then he started taking all he could get.

Maxi stuffed gumdrops into his pockets. He put lollipops in his shirt. He put peppermint and gingerbread into his cap until it ran over. Maxi was behaving like a pig.

"MAXI MUFFIN!" Mini said angrily. "What will the Pippins think of you? And what does Jesus think of you?"

Maxi stopped. He wanted to please Jesus by what he did. But he also wanted to please Jesus by what he did NOT do.

"I . . . I'm sorry I let Greedy Maxi take so much," Maxi said. "I really must talk with him about this. Jesus is much more pleased with Thankful Maxi. Thank you, thank you for these wonderful gifts."

Mini smiled as Maxi put most of the lollipops, gumdrops, gingerbread and peppermint back. Then the Pippins waved good-bye to Mini and Thankful Maxi.

So Maxi and Mini sailed back home on The Golden Tub, blown by the winds of imagination.

# Growing Is . . .
# Doing Good for Jesus

### What the Bible Story Teaches
If we want to be Jesus' friend we must give up bad things in our lives.

### Thinking about the Bible Story
1. Why didn't Zacchaeus have any friends?
2. What did Zacchaeus do that was wrong?
3. How did Zacchaeus change when he met Jesus?

### What the Muffin Story Teaches
Jesus is ashamed of us when we do something bad.

### Thinking about the Muffin Story
1. Why was Mini ashamed of the way Maxi took so much candy?
2. Why was Jesus ashamed of that too?
3. What did Maxi do to change that? Why was Jesus pleased to see Maxi change?

# What Would Jesus Think?

Which would Jesus be pleased or ashamed for you to do:

1. Call your mother a bad name.
2. Pull your cat's tail.
3. Put chewing gum in a friend's hair.
4. Tell a friend that Jesus loves her.
5. Memorize a Bible verse.

## What the Bible Says

*Jesus said, "If you are ashamed of Me, I will be ashamed of you"* (from Luke 9:26).

## Prayer

Dear Jesus, please don't be ashamed of me. Show me what to do so that You will be pleased with me. Amen.

# Pleasing Jesus by Yes and No

**Matthew 21:28-32**

The Pharisees often made trouble for Jesus. They thought Jesus was just a man. When He said He was God's Son, they hated Him.

One day Jesus told them a story. It was about a father and two sons. But it was really a story about these Pharisees:

One morning a father asked his son, "Will you help me in our vineyard?"

"No," said the son. "I want to have some fun with my friends."

The father was sorry that his son said no. So he asked his other son.

"Yes," said the other son.

The father was happy to hear this. Why couldn't his first son be like this one?

But when the father went to the vineyard, there was the son who said no. The son who said yes was gone.

"Where is your brother?" the father asked.

"He went away to have fun with some friends," said the son.

"But you said you were going away," said the father.

"I know, but I saw how wrong I was," said the son. "So I've come to help you."

The son who said no at first helped his father. The son who said yes did not.

"Which son obeyed his father?" Jesus asked the Pharisees.

"The first," they said.

"But you are like the other son," Jesus told them. You must please God by obeying Him, not by what you SAY you do for Him."

That's good for us to remember, isn't it?

# Pleasing by Obeying

"Poppi, look!" said Maxi. "I've taught Ruff to obey."

"Sit!" said Maxi. Ruff sat down.

"Stay!" said Maxi. Ruff would not move.

"Come Ruff!" said Maxi. Ruff ran to him.

"Very good," said Poppi. "You've done a good job. Ruff has too."

"Yep, any dog of mine is going to obey or else," said Maxi.

"Or else what?" Poppi asked with a grin.

"Just or else," said Maxi.

Poppi went inside while Maxi stayed out to play with Ruff. It didn't seem long before Mommi opened the door and called to Maxi. "Dinner!" she said. "Come quickly."

"OK," said Maxi. "Coming."

But Maxi was having so much fun with Ruff that he wanted to try a few more "sits," "stays," and "come Ruffs."

Mommi put dinner on the table. Everyone sat down to eat. Everyone but Maxi.

Mommi opened the door again. "Maxi!" she said. "We're all at the table. Come now!"

"Coming!" Maxi said. But he was having too much fun with Ruff.

"Next time you call him," Mommi said to Poppi when she came back.

A few minutes later Poppi went to the door. But when he saw Maxi playing he had another idea.

"Here, Ruff! Come here!" he called.

Ruff ran across the lawn, and hurried into the house with Poppi. Now Maxi had no one to play with, so he washed and came to the table. But was Maxi surprised! There was Ruff, sitting in his chair, puffing happily.

"What's that dog doing in my chair?" Maxi asked.

"Any dog of ours is going to obey," said Poppi. "Ruff obeyed, so he's at the table instead of you."

"But . . . but I did say I was coming," said Maxi softly.

"Hmmmm. You said you were coming but didn't. Ruff didn't say he was coming, but he came," said Poppi. "I'll let you decide who obeyed. But while you're deciding tell Ruff to get off your chair so you can eat."

Of course Ruff obeyed. So did Maxi, whenever he could remember. And so will you, whenever you remember this story.

# Growing Is . . . Doing Good Things

### What the Bible Story Teaches
It's not enough to say that you will please Jesus, you must also do it.

### Thinking about the Bible Story
1. Which son said he would help his father? Why didn't he?
2. How did the other son help his father?
3. Which was best, to say "I will" but don't or to say "I won't" and do it?
4. Would it be even better to say "yes, I will help" and do it? Why?

### What the Muffin Story Teaches
Don't just say you will obey. Do it!

### Thinking about the Muffin Story
1. Who obeyed better, Maxi or Ruff?
2. What would you like to tell Maxi when he said he wanted Ruff to obey him?
3. Do you obey your parents? Do you obey Jesus?

# How Do You Obey?

Mommi tells you each of these. Which would you obey?

1. Do your homework.
2. Clean up your room.
3. Help with the dishes.
4. Feed your dog or cat.

## What the Bible Says

*Children, obey your parents* (from Ephesians 6:1).

## Prayer

Dear Jesus, I want to obey my parents because You want me to do it. Amen.

# GROWING UP
## TO PRAISE JESUS

# A Day to Praise Jesus

**Matthew 21:1-11,14-17**

"You will find a little donkey in that village over there," Jesus told two friends. "Bring it to me."

"But the man who owns it will ask what we are doing," they said.

"Tell the owner that I need it," Jesus answered.

The friends walked to the village and found the little donkey where Jesus said it would be. "How does Jesus know this donkey is here?" they wondered. "How does He know the owner will let Him use it?"

When the friends untied the donkey someone shouted. "Stop! What are you doing?"

"Jesus needs it," they said.

"Jesus? Of course! Take it," the man said.

When the two returned they threw their cloaks on the donkey's back and helped Jesus get up. Then Jesus began riding toward Jerusalem.

Crowds gathered quickly around Jesus. They always did wherever He went. But today it was different. People usually begged Jesus to heal them. Today they began to praise Him.

"The king of Israel will ride into Jerusalem on a donkey," someone shouted.

"Hosanna!" shouted others. "Blessed is

the One who comes in the name of the Lord."

Before long the air was filled with shouts of "Hosanna! Hosanna in the highest!"

As the donkey moved toward Jerusalem more people joined the crowd. "Hosanna!" the people kept shouting.

"What's happening?" some asked.

"A new king for Israel," said others.

People began to throw their cloaks in front of Jesus. Others cut branches and laid them in His path. Children shouted. Mothers and fathers waved their hands. The air was filled with joy.

The Pharisees and their friends were not filled with joy. "Stop those people from saying such things," they said to Jesus.

"If I do, the stones will shout praises," Jesus said. "The Bible says this will happen, so it must happen."

It was a day to praise Jesus. Don't you wish you could have been there? Don't you wish you could have praised Jesus too?

# A Way to Praise Jesus

"The Great Tent Meeting is about to begin," said Pookie.

"Why are you the preacher?" Maxi asked.

"Because I was first," said Pookie.

How could Maxi argue with that?

"La-dees and gentlemen," Pookie began. It seemed a safe way to begin. Maxi couldn't argue with that either.

"If you come up here and become a Christian your troubles will all be over," Pookie shouted.

"That's not true!" Maxi interrupted. Pookie, BoBo, Mini, and Maria all stared at Maxi. They had never heard anyone interrupt a Great Tent Meeting before.

"Why isn't it true?" Pookie argued.

"Because I'm a Christian and my pet frog died," said Maxi. "And Ruff is sick."

"I have an idea," said Mini. "Let's talk with Mrs. Murgatroyd. She's a Christian and is sick a lot."

So the Great Tent Meeting went to Mrs. Murgatroyd's house. "Why doesn't Jesus take your sickness away," Maxi asked.

"I asked that many times," said Mrs. Murgatroyd. "Then I found the answer. Since I can't go to church I call others and ask them to go. Fifteen families go to church today because I can't go. I don't want to be sick, but since I am, I'm glad I can praise Jesus this way."

"Wow," said Pookie. "So you're praising Jesus with your sickness rather than grumbling to Him about it. Let's go back to the Great Tent Meeting. I've got a new sermon about praising Jesus."

# Growing Is . . . Praising Jesus

### What the Bible Story Teaches

Do you like to praise Jesus? If you love Him, you will.

### Thinking about the Bible Story

1. How did the people praise Jesus?
2. Should they have done this? Why?
3. Why would you like to have been there that day?

### What the Muffin Story Teaches

We can praise Jesus, even when we are sick or have problems.

### Thinking about the Muffin Story

1. Will Jesus take away all our troubles? Why not? What did Pookie say at first? Why did Maxi not like that?
2. Did Jesus take away Mrs. Murgatroyd's sickness? How did she praise Jesus when she was sick?
3. If you have some troubles, ask how you can praise Jesus anyway.

# Praising Jesus
# When I Have Troubles

Which of these do you think are true?

1. If my pet dies, I can praise Jesus by asking Him to comfort me.
2. If my poppi loses his job, I can praise Jesus by asking Him to help my poppi.
3. If I get sick for a few days, I can praise Jesus by asking Him to help me use my time well.

## The Bible Says

*It is good for God's people to praise Him* (from Psalm 33:1).

## Prayer

I want to praise You, dear Jesus, because You are wonderful. I want to praise You because You do wonderful things for me. Amen.

# How to Make the Angels Happy

**Luke 15:8-10**

A Story Jesus Told

There was once a woman who had ten coins. It may not sound like much money. But it was all she could save. Each coin was worth what a man earned for a day's work.

The woman kept her ten silver coins in a jar hidden in her house. She liked to take the jar from its hiding place and look at the coins. Some day she would need those coins!

But one day when she took the jar down and began to count her coins she cried out. She counted again and again. But she could find only nine silver coins.

"Oh, no," she said. "I had ten coins. But one of them is lost."

The woman ran to find a lamp. It looked like a little covered gravy dish with a wick in one end. It was filled with olive oil.

The woman lit her lamp and looked in every corner of the room. But she could not find her lost coin.

Next she got her broom and swept every part of the room. Suddenly the broom sent something spinning across the floor.

"My coin!" the woman cried out. "I have found it."

The woman was so happy. Then she ran out and told her neighbors the good news. They were very, very happy with her.

"The angels of God are just as happy when a person follows Me," Jesus said. Do you have a friend who doesn't know Jesus? You will make the angels happy if you help your friend follow Jesus. That's worth doing, isn't it?

# Praising Jesus for Something Special

"Oh, Mommi, this is the most beautiful gold charm I have ever had," Mini crooned. "I just LOVE it."

"I'm glad you do, Mini," said Mommi. "Your grandmommi gave it to me when I was a girl your age. I decided you're old enough now to have it."

"But it's so tiny," said Mini.

"Yes, as soon as Poppi comes home, we'll ask him to put it on your charm bracelet," Mommi added. "Until then be careful. It would be easy to lose."

"Oh, I won't lose it," said Mini. "I'll hold it tight all day."

Mini did hold it tight. That is, until she realized that she wasn't holding it tight.

"But I had it right here in my hand," Mini whispered to herself. "Where did it go?"

Mini looked at the sofa where she had been sitting. It could have fallen between the cushions. But she had also walked into her room. It could be anywhere in the rug.

"I must run downtown to do some chores, Mini," Mommi called from the kitchen. "I'll be back in a couple of hours."

When Mini heard the door slam, she took all the cushions from the sofa and moved her hand along the back.

"Two hours," she said. "I must find that charm before Mommi comes home. What will I tell her if I don't?"

Mini was sure she had looked at every inch of that sofa. Then she put the cushions on again.

Next she got on her hands and knees and began to feel in the rug. She spread the rug apart as she crawled along. Mini was sure she looked in every tiny piece of rug between the sofa and her room. She was sure it must also be time for Mommi to come home.

By the time Mini reached her room, the tears were streaming down her cheeks. She looked in her jewelry box. She even looked in the pockets of her clothes in the closet.

Mini was frantic now. She could not find her beautiful antique charm anywhere.

Mini plopped on her bed and cried as if her heart would break. What would she tell Mommi?

Suddenly Mini's hand felt something. She looked toward her hand.

"MY CHARM!" Mini shouted. "MY CHARM! MY CHARM! MY CHARM! I found it."

Just then the door opened and Mini ran into Mommi's and Poppi's arms. She was bubbling with excitement.

"I FOUND IT! I FOUND IT!" she shouted.

"Let me guess," said Poppi. "A million dollars? No wait! It's two million."

"Oh, Poppi, no, more than that!" said Mini.

"Three million," said Poppi. "I won't go higher than that."

Mini giggled. "I lost the beautiful charm Mommi gave me. Now I've found it. Can I invite some friends over for ice cream. I'm so happy that I want to tell them about it."

"OK, Mini," said Mommi. "But first let's ask Poppi to put the charm on your bracelet."

It was a CHARM-ing party Mini had. And Mommi said it reminded her of the Bible story of the woman who lost her coin. What do you think?

# Growing Is . . . Rejoicing

### What the Bible Story Teaches
Even the angels rejoice when you help someone know Jesus.

### Thinking about the Bible Story
1. Why was the woman in this story so happy?
2. Why were the neighbors happy? It wasn't their coin!
3. When do angels rejoice? Have you helped some angels rejoice by telling a friend about Jesus? Will you?

### What the Muffin Story Teaches
We should rejoice with each other.

### Thinking about the Muffin Story
1. Why was Mini so happy to find her charm?
2. Why did she want some friends to come for ice cream? What did she want them to do?
3. Do you rejoice when something good happens to a friend? Do your friends rejoice when something good happens to you?
4. Why should we rejoice with each other?

# Rejoicing about Jesus

Which of these show joy for what Jesus has done?

1. Singing songs about Jesus.
2. Saying good things about Jesus.
3. Making fun of Jesus' friends.
4. Doing good things for Jesus.

## What the Bible Says

*I want to show joy, even when I have problems* (from 2 Corinthians 7:4).

## Prayer

Dear Jesus, You know that I sometimes have problems. Teach me how to rejoice, even when those problems come. Amen.